Thank you!

BELMONT COUNTY DISTRICT LIBRARY
Purchased with funds from the
November 2013 Library Levy

JUMPING SPIDERS

Joanne Randolph

PowerKiDS
press™

New York

Published in 2014 by The Rosen Publishing Group, Inc.
29 East 21st Street, New York, NY 10010

First Edition

Editor: Jennifer Way and Norman D. Graubart
Book Design: Andrew Povolny
Photo Research: Katie Stryker

Photo Credits: Cover Thomas Shahan/Flickr/Getty Images; pp. 4, 10, 14 (bottom) Kurt_G/Shutterstock.com; p. 5 iStockphoto/Thinkstock; p. 6 Warin Keawchookul/Shutterstock.com; p. 7 Gucio_55/Shutterstock.com; p. 8 Last Refuge/Robert Harding World Imagery/Getty Images; p. 9 D. Kucharski K. Kucharaska/Shutterstock.com; p. 11 Cathy Keifer/Shutterstock.com; pp. 12–13 Krom1975/Shutterstock.com; p. 14 (top) Carol Farneti-Foster/Oxford Scientific/Getty Images; pp. 15, 21 Henrik Larsson/Shutterstock.com; p. 16 Visuals Unlimited, Inc./Fabio Pupin/Getty Images; p. 17 (top) Nature's Images/Photo Researchers/Getty Images; p. 17 (bottom) up close with nature/Flickr/Getty Images pp. 18–19 Tomatito/Shutterstock.com; p. 20 Frank Greenaway/Dorling Kindersley/Getty Images; p. 22 Steve Satushek/Botanica/Getty Images.

Library of Congress Cataloging-in-Publication Data

Randolph, Joanne, author.
  Jumping spiders / by Joanne Randolph.
      pages cm. — (Nightmare creatures. Spiders!)
  Includes index.
  ISBN 978-1-4777-2889-5 (library) — ISBN 978-1-4777-2978-6 (pbk.) —
ISBN 978-1-4777-3048-5 (6-pack)
  1. Jumping spiders—Juvenile literature. I. Title.
  QL458.42.S24R36 2014
  595.4'4—dc23
                              2013022318

Manufactured in the United States of America

CPSIA Compliance Information: Batch #W14PK6: For Further Information contact Rosen Publishing, New York, New York at 1-800-237-9932

CONTENTS

MEET THE JUMPING SPIDER

Imagine a spider that seems to be staring straight at you. That sounds kind of creepy, doesn't it? It may be a jumping spider. The jumping spider family is the largest family of spiders in the world. There are 5,000 known **species** of jumping spiders. The jumping spider belongs to the Salticidae family. They are called jumping spiders because they can jump high and far.

The fringed jumping spider probably has the longest jump of any jumping spider. It can jump 47 times its own body length.

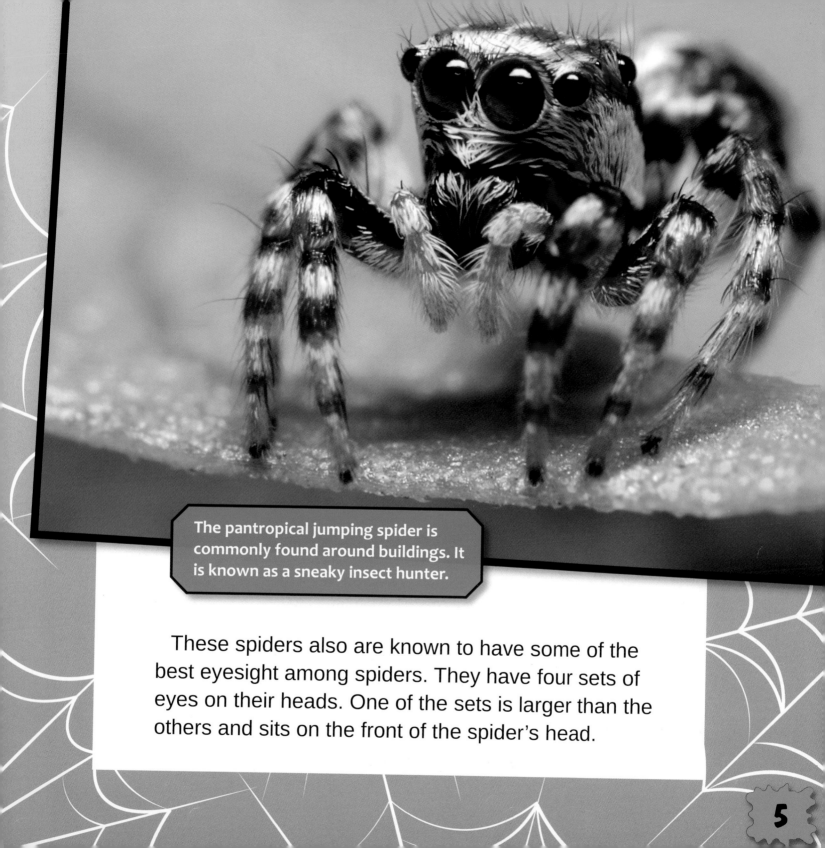

The pantropical jumping spider is commonly found around buildings. It is known as a sneaky insect hunter.

These spiders also are known to have some of the best eyesight among spiders. They have four sets of eyes on their heads. One of the sets is larger than the others and sits on the front of the spider's head.

WHERE ARE THEY?

Jumping spiders are found everywhere in the world except the polar regions. They also make their homes in many different **habitats**. Most species are found living near the equator in **tropical** forests, but not all of them live there. There are plenty of jumping spiders in **temperate** forests, deserts, along coasts, and on mountainsides. There are probably jumping spiders living near you!

This is a jumping spider next to its silky shelter. Shelters are like webs, except that they are not built for catching prey.

Wooded forests are common places for jumping spiders to make their homes.

Wherever a jumping spider lives, it makes a special home for itself. Jumping spiders do not use their silk to spin webs. They do use it to make tentlike shelters. They use these shelters to keep safe from weather, to sleep, to lay and store their eggs, and to **molt**. Molting is when an animal sheds its skin.

Jumping spiders are easy to tell apart from other kinds of spiders. As with all spiders, their heads and thoraxes are fused together. Two sets of their eight eyes are on the fronts of their heads. They also have large, strong legs. The front two pairs of legs are generally larger than the back two sets.

Jumping spiders can stretch their legs very far. This helps them jump long distances.

8

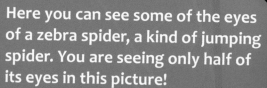
Here you can see some of the eyes of a zebra spider, a kind of jumping spider. You are seeing only half of its eyes in this picture!

As do all spiders, jumping spiders have two main body parts. These are the head and the **abdomen**. The jumping spider's eight legs are attached to the head. The parts that make silk, called **spinnerets**, are at the back of the abdomen.

JUMP TO KILL

Many other kinds of spiders spin their webs and then wait for dinner to get caught. Jumping spiders do not wait for a web to do all of the work. They are active hunters. They use their excellent eyesight to track **prey**. They quietly sneak up on it. They get themselves ready and then spring into action.

This brown jumping spider has a line of silk coming out of its spinneret.

This jumping spider is eating a cricket. Crickets are a common meal for jumping spiders.

Some species of jumping spiders can jump up to nearly 50 times their body lengths. They often attach safety lines of silk to whatever they are jumping from. If all goes well, they won't need it, and instead will be snacking on an **insect**.

NIGHTMARE FACTS

1. Have you heard people say that mothers have eyes on the backs of their heads? Well, jumping spiders really do! It is hard for prey to get past these spiders.

2. Some jumping spiders feed mainly on other spiders. Fringed jumping spiders even eat other spiders' eggs.

3. Some jumping spiders can learn and remember colors. This makes them better hunters.

4. All jumping spiders are carnivores, or meat eaters, including those that eat mostly nectar and plants.

5. Jumping spider **venom paralyzes** the prey. It also works to turn everything inside the bug to a liquid.

6. Male jumping spiders must do a **courtship** dance when they come near a female. If not, the female might treat the male as an enemy and try to eat it.

13

WHAT'S FOR DINNER?

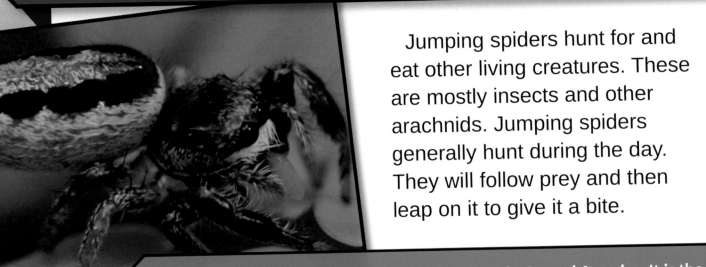

Jumping spiders hunt for and eat other living creatures. These are mostly insects and other arachnids. Jumping spiders generally hunt during the day. They will follow prey and then leap on it to give it a bite.

Above: The *Bagheera kiplingi* jumping spider lives in Central America. It is the only jumping spider that eats mostly plants instead of insects.

Below: One kind of insect jumping spiders often eat is a leafhopper. Leafhoppers can make a soft, vibrating sound to startle predators and attempt escape.

Vampire spiders can smell if a mosquito has recently drunk blood. These spiders prefer blood-filled mosquitoes, such as the one above.

Their venom quickly paralyzes the bug so the jumping spider can eat before the prey gets away.

Some kinds of jumping spiders will eat most any bug that comes along. Others are pickier. Some species will eat mainly ants, moths, or other spiders. The vampire spider prefers mosquitoes, for example. There are a few species of hunting spiders that have been known to eat nectar or plant matter in addition to insects.

DANCING, EGGS, AND BABIES

Jumping spiders are generally solitary. This means they spend most of their time alone. The only time they come together is to **mate**. Males are more brightly colored than females, with shiny, colorful hair and body parts. They flash these parts during courtship dances for the female. These dances include moving sideways or in zigzag patterns, among other patterns.

These two spiders are of the same species. The one on the left is a female, while the right one is a male.

This spider is called a daring jumping spider. These spiders live all over the United States and in parts of Canada and Mexico.

New studies have also found that males make buzzing and drumroll sounds to attract females. If the female is interested, they mate.

The female will put more than 100 eggs in her silken shelter. She guards these eggs until they hatch.

Some female jumping spiders stay with their eggs to protect them while others hide them in silk and then leave.

17

READY, SET, FIGHT!

Before male jumping spiders even get to the courting dance, they need to make it through a fight! Male jumping spiders will fight over which spider gets to mate with a female. Often males follow special smells made by the female.

When a spider senses danger or is about to fight, it puts its two front legs in the air. These two jumping spiders are about to fight.

When they find a shelter, the smell will let them know whether there is a female of mating age inside or not. The males wait for her to molt and choose a mate. While they wait, they pass the time by fighting. The male that wins gets to do his dance for the female.

Female jumping spiders fight over mates, too. Though these fights happen less often, females often fight to the death!

WATCH OUT, JUMPING SPIDER!

All spiders serve as dinner for other species. The jumping spider is no different. Jumping spiders look like a yummy meal to many birds, spiders, and insects, such as the praying mantis and the spider wasp.

Jumping spiders do not make homes in webs, so spider wasps can often catch them without getting caught in traps.

This jumping spider is hiding very well.

Just as the jumping spider's excellent eyesight helps it hunt, it also helps it see and avoid **predators**. The spider's colors also generally help it blend with its surroundings. This is called **camouflage**. If predators come too close, the spider can jump away to safety, too.

You can try to spot jumping spiders in their natural habitat. Watch what they do and take some notes. If you see a zebra spider, it might look back at you. These jumping spiders are known for their ability to recognize humans.

You will soon see that jumping spiders are not the creatures of nightmares at all. They are skilled hunters with an important part to play in our world.

This backyard explorer has found a spider in its web. You may find jumping spiders in your backyard, too.

GLOSSARY

abdomen (AB-duh-mun) The large, rear part of an insect's or arachnid's body.

camouflage (KA-muh-flahj) A color or shape that matches what is around something and helps hide it.

courtship (KORT-ship) The period of activity before a male and female make babies.

habitats (HA-buh-tats) The surroundings where animals or plants naturally live.

insect (IN-sekt) A small animal that often has six legs and wings.

mate (MAYT) To come together to make babies.

molt (MOHLT) To shed hair, feathers, shell, horns, or skin.

paralyzes (PA-ruh-lyz-ez) Takes away feeling or movement.

predators (PREH-duh-terz) Animals that kill other animals for food.

prey (PRAY) An animal that is hunted by another animal for food.

species (SPEE-sheez) One kind of living thing. All people are one species.

spinnerets (spih-nuh-RETS) Parts, located on the rear of the spider's body, that make silk.

temperate (TEM-puh-rut) Not too hot or too cold.

tropical (TRAH-puh-kul) Having to do with the warm parts of Earth that are near the equator.

venom (VEH-num) A poison passed by one animal into another through a bite or a sting.

INDEX

WEBSITES

Due to the changing nature of Internet links, PowerKids Press has developed an online list of websites related to the subject of this book. This site is updated regularly. Please use this link to access the list: www.powerkidslinks.com/ncs/jump/